CW00470410

ACCESSING THE **SUPERNATURAL** THROUGH ...

# SPEAKING IN TONGUES

## John Edwards

Foreword by Dr. Mark Virkler

# CONTENTS

# FOREWORD

This booklet by John Edwards gives a wonderful over-view of the gift of speaking in tongues. Many of us, including me, have held a wide range of views about speaking in tongues.

Initially I was taught that speaking in tongues was not for our time, so I rejected it and I rejected anyone who spoke in tongues. However, Derek Prince's teaching convinced me that speaking in tongues is relevant for today, and it would be of great value in my life. After all, God gives **good** gifts, and I desire anything that God offers.

In light of this, I fasted, pursued God and went to an evening service where they laid hands on my wife Patti and me to receive the baptism in the Holy Spirit and the gift of speaking in tongues. I expected God to take my tongue and move it around and He didn't. Patti received the gift and I didn't. I became very depressed because I had experienced nothing.

A couple of weeks later I sat in the rocking chair in my living room reading Acts 2:4, and I noticed something I had never seen before: THEY spoke as the Spirit gave them utterance. There are two parts to this miracle. **They** did the **speaking** and the **Spirit gave the utterance**.

I realized in a flash that I was waiting for God to do both parts of this miracle. I wanted Him to "do the speaking" (i.e. take my tongue and move it around), and to provide the syllables which would be spoken. He was revealing to me that He would provide syllables but I was the one who needed to decide to speak them out.

He also showed me that the Holy Spirit is the River of God Who flows from the throne of God and FLOWS within me (Jn. 7:37-39), so when I tune in to the Spirit, I also need to tune in to the flow within That was a BIG revelation. Until the moment that I received this revelation, I had possessed no theology concerning flow. I lived completely in analytical reasoning, the way that my culture had taught me to live, and that was what I was most comfortable doing.

So with these two revelations, I again asked for the baptism in the Holy Spirit and the gift of speaking in tongues. I tuned in to flow and choose to speak. That means I chose to begin articulating sounds while not consciously forming the syllables.

My analytical mind listened to the syllables and instantly decided "gibberish." Of course my mind considers all other languages gibberish simply because it doesn't understand them. So now it was time to take the next step. I needed to take every thought captive to the obedience of Christ (2 Cor. 10:5). I told my mind to "stop it" and that "speaking in tongues was my spirit praying and this is designed to build up my spirit and not to inform my mind" (1 Cor. 14:2,4). So this next step was a step of faith.

I needed to **choose to believe** that what God says in the Bible is true and that I can live the Bible. There is a River. The River does flow. When I tune to flow I am tuning to the River that flows within me. When I speak flowing syllables, I am speaking in tongues. How do I know? I know because when I ask according to His will (1 Cor. 14:5) I know that He hears me and I have the request I have made known to Him (1 Jn. 5:14,15). My emotions screamed, "But I don't feel anything." My response was, "You don't need to. There is no verse in the Bible that says I need to feel emotions when I speak in tongues."

So there you have it: 1) **We ask** for the Holy Spirit to come upon us, 2) **We yield** from self-control to Spirit-control – from syllables controlled by my brain to **flowing syllables**, 3) **We speak forth these syllables**, 4) **We believe** the Bible is true and the **flow within** us is the River of the Holy Spirit which flows from God's throne. Try it. You'll like it!

And yes, my emotions did eventually come on board with this all. I repented for scorning emotions as soulish and having no value and asked God to restore them to me. I learned that emotions are a byproduct of whatever I am gazing upon. I realized I could gaze upon a heavenly scene of myself worshipping before His throne with the heavenly host, and then when speaking in tongues, Kingdom emotions would flood my heart: emotions of love, joy, peace, mercy, compassion.

Again I say, "Try it, You'll like it."

The Bible became real to me as I realized "I can live the Bible." My Christian faith came alive in a whole new way. Talk about exciting!

As you read this booklet, you will receive a solid biblical understanding of the Baptism in the Holy Spirit and the gift of speaking in tongues, so by all means read on, and for heaven's sake, "Try it. You'll like it."

Peace

Dr. Mark Virkler
Founder of *Communion With God Ministries*

# INTRODUCTION

As a lad of fifteen, I readily joined the group who had responded to the invitation given at the close of the Sunday evening service – an invitation to seek and receive the baptism in the Holy Spirit. A visiting speaker was preaching at the church that I, with my family, had attended all my life. He challenged the congregation with the promise God had given in His Word to pour out His Spirit on all flesh. My heart was stirred to receive all that was available. In a large room at the rear of the main hall, we gathered with the speaker. He encouraged us to believe what God had said: that the Holy Spirit was poured out, and by faith, we could receive Him. As hands were laid on us all, I began, in my heart, to thank the Lord for my salvation and to tell Jesus how much I loved Him. We all had been encouraged to "drink in the Holy Spirit," and I was seeking to do this. That evening I was filled with the Holy Spirit, and I began to "speak in tongues," as under the anointing of God's Spirit I spoke out that which He was prompting within. Since that Sunday evening in London, now more than thirty years ago, I have continued to exercise the gift of speaking in tongues. In times of joy and in times of sorrow, in worship and in intercession, when rejoicing in God and when calling out for the Lord's help, it is a gift that is of daily benefit. I have found the Holy Spirit to be the Comforter and His presence the "well of water springing up." God in His wisdom has ordained that the manifestation, the bursting forth of the Holy Spirit in "other tongues," be the means of great blessing for all who are born again by faith in Jesus.

In this book, I have sought to show in a practical way the value and wonder of the gift of tongues. I have included personal experiences and also those of other people that I hope will illustrate the value of tongues.

CHAPTER 1

# INCIDENCES OF SPEAKING IN TONGUES IN THE NEW TESTAMENT

**THE DAY OF PENTECOST** (ACTS 2:1-39)

Fifty days after the Passover when Jesus was crucified, and a little over a week from the time His disciples had seen Him as the risen Savior, taken up into heaven, those same disciples were meeting together. They had gathered in anticipation of the outpouring of the gift of the Holy Spirit, the Comforter they had been promised. Jesus had often spoken to them of the Holy Spirit, and His last words to them before ascending to heaven had been, *"You will receive power when the Holy Spirit comes on you"* (Acts 1:8). Suddenly, there was a sound like a violent wind blowing and they saw what appeared to be flames of fire that separated and came to each of them. The waiting believers were at that moment filled with the Holy Spirit, and they began to speak in languages which were not their own and of which they had no previous understanding. Even as they spoke, they were not aware of the meaning of the words they let pour from their lips as, from their hearts, they magnified and praised the Lord.

That these words which poured forth were indeed languages was acknowledged by many in the crowd that came together, attracted by the noisy, uninhibited praise of the disciples. From provinces of the Roman and Parthian Empires were visitors to Jerusalem, who could hear their own language among those being spoken out. They said that the disciples were *"declaring the wonders of God"* (Acts 2:11). This manifestation of the Holy Spirit, generally known as *"speaking in tongues"* (from the wording in the Authorized Version of the Bible) is not known in Scripture before the day of Pentecost, when the disciples were baptized in the Holy Spirit. However, from that time on, speaking in tongues is mentioned. In the Acts of the Apostles, it is seen as a sign accompanying the receiving of the Holy Spirit. In the Epistles, it is shown to be a spiritual gift exercised by Christians in their private worship and also when they meet together as believers for worship and fellowship (when a message in tongues can be interpreted for the benefit of all present).

### PETER AND CORNELIUS (ACTS 10:1-48)

The apostle Peter was directed to the house of Cornelius, a centurion in the Roman army, to tell him the way of salvation. Although he was a God-fearing man, Cornelius was a Gentile, and Peter, a devout Jew, would normally have shunned any social contact with him. In that Gentile home, as Peter testified of Jesus and the forgiveness of sins through His name, Cornelius, with the relatives and close friends he had called together to hear Peter, received the gift of the Holy Spirit, and they began to speak in tongues and praise God. Peter and those who had visited the home with him were astonished that the Gentiles were able to receive the gift of God, just as the Jews who believed in Jesus had. Hearing Cornelius and his friends speaking in tongues convinced Peter that they had received the same Holy Spirit that he had received, and that it was the same infilling the disciples had known on the day of Pentecost. He realized that it was God's intention to save the Gentiles as well as the Jews through faith in Jesus, and that the gift of the Holy Spirit was for all.

**PAUL AT EPHESUS** (ACTS 19:1-7)
On his third missionary journey, the apostle Paul visited Ephesus, a commercial center and the most important city in western Asia Minor. There he met a group of about twenty men who had received the teaching of John the Baptist. Accepting the message from Paul that Jesus was the Savior whom John the Baptist had announced was to come, these men were baptized in water, and then, after Paul had placed his hands on them, *"the Holy Spirit came on them, and they spoke in tongues and prophesied"* (Acts 19:6).

CHAPTER 2

# WHAT IS SPEAKING IN TONGUES?

The New Testament term "speaking in tongues" refers to the ability to speak by the inspiration of the Holy Spirit in a language that has not been learned and that which is not understood by the person speaking. These languages are sometimes recognized by those who hear them, but generally this is not the case. Paul's reference to *"the tongues of men and of angels"* (1 Corinthians 13:1), may indicate that languages other than human may be inspired by the Holy Spirit.

## WHAT IS THE POINT?

To the natural mind, speaking in a language you do not understand makes no sense at all. Imagine going out into your town and stopping someone on the street to tell him you can speak in a language which you have never learned. That person would probably look at you rather strangely. If you then followed your first claim by explaining that while you were speaking that language, you did not understand what you were saying, the bemused citizen would probably beat a hasty retreat. "I see no point in tongues, so it's not for me." Such a statement can be understood from the non-Christian, but Christians are to be led by God's Word. The encouragement of Scripture is that all believers should seek to speak in tongues (1 Corinthians 14:5), and that the use of the gift should not be forbidden (1 Corinthians 14:39). Some Christians have dismissed the gift of tongues because they have not understood its value and significance. They therefore deprive themselves and those they influence of much blessing.

**THE APOSTLE PAUL'S INSTRUCTIONS ON TONGUES**
Part of the apostle Paul's first Epistle to the Corinthians deals with spiritual gifts and the mature and orderly use of these gifts in Christian gatherings. His desire is that believers should not be ignorant of spiritual gifts (1 Corinthians 12:1). All nine gifts listed in this passage are manifestations of the one Holy Spirit, and the distribution of these gifts to the believers is at the discretion of the Holy Spirit. The nine gifts listed in 1 Corinthians 12:7-10 are often categorized as three power gifts (healings, miracles, faith), three knowledge gifts (word of knowledge, word of wisdom, discerning of spirits), and three utterance gifts (prophecy, tongues, interpretation of tongues). The Holy Spirit distributes these gifts as He wills (1 Corinthians 12:11), yet it seems that He delights to give the utterance gifts, in particular, to all who seek them. The Scriptures teach that we may all

prophesy (1 Corinthians 14:5, 31, 39), and they encourage all believers to speak in tongues and to pray for the interpretation of tongues (1 Corinthians 14:13). Paul obviously considered speaking in tongues a necessary and valuable exercise in his prayer life, for he claims to speak in tongues more than any of the believers in the church at Corinth (1 Corinthians 14:18). The church at Corinth was not hesitant in the use of spiritual gifts – he had to caution them for being too enthusiastic. Considering Paul's education in the things of God, his calling, and his abundant revelation in spiritual truth, that he should be so ardent in his speaking in tongues is an indication of how necessary the gift is to the spiritual life of every Christian. Sadly, some Christians despise speaking in tongues or consider it unnecessary, because they have never realized the value of the gift or they have been taught that it is not for today.

## THE LOSS OF THE SPIRITUAL GIFTS

After the early centuries of growth in the Church, there came a time of spiritual dearth and falling away from the true life of God – the 'dark ages' of the Church. Most of the churches were linked with secular powers, resulting in the truths of salvation being corrupted and the life of the Spirit being extinguished. However, throughout the history of the Church, there was a record of believers who exercised the gift of speaking in tongues, including such notable men as John Wesley, Charles Finney and D.L. Moody. (Finney described his experiences as 'unutterable gushings'). This century has seen an outpouring of the Holy Spirit on a remarkable, world-wide scale. Many millions of believers throughout the world are experiencing the baptism in the Holy Spirit, and as a result they are speaking in tongues and have a new understanding of life in the Holy Spirit. The life of the early Church, with its power and demonstration of the dynamic and life of God's kingdom, is in evidence in the world again. Perhaps this is the latter rain spoken of in the Scriptures, which are to lead up to the return of Jesus.

CHAPTER 3

# THE VALUE OF TONGUES TO THE INDIVIDUAL BELIEVER: PART 1

**SPIRITUAL EDIFICATION**

Man is made up of spirit, soul and body. Paul in his letter to the Thessalonians prays that their *"whole spirit, soul and body be kept blameless at the coming of our Lord Jesus Christ"* (1 Thessalonians 5:23). Just as our physical body needs to be kept strong and healthy, so also does the inner man. The body needs food and physical exercise. When either is lacking, it soon shows. In a similar way, our soul life – our mind and emotions – need to be stimulated and fed. We value the exchange of ideas, reading, conversation, meeting with friends, and fellowship with other Christians.

What then of the spirit man – that which can have direct fellowship and communion with the Lord? Speaking in tongues is an activity of our spirit. First Corinthians 14:14 shows us that when someone prays in other tongues, it is directly from his spirit – his "spirit prays." In verse 2 of the same chapter, Paul explains that when someone *"speaks in tongues... he utters mysteries with his spirit."*

Paul writes, *"he who speaks in a tongue edifies himself"* (1 Corinthians 14:4); he is "building up' his spirit." This is important for Christians, who are to be *"led by the Spirit"* rather than dominated by their emotions (the soulish) or controlled by their physical appetites (the carnal Christian).

The daily use of tongues in worship and prayer will keep the spirit strong. If a man were only to eat food on Sunday, by Monday evening, he would be feeling hungry; by Wednesday, he would be famished; and by Saturday he'd be on his knees. Daily nourishment is vital for normal living. The serious athlete needs to practice his discipline daily. How strange it would be for a man to have a good chat with his wife on Sunday and then say, "that was most rewarding; I'll talk to you again next Sunday." Yet so many Christians only build themselves up in their spirit when they meet for worship on Sunday. It is no surprise that their spirit seems weak, and they lack spiritual stamina and understanding. Daily speaking in tongues is a good practical way of building up the spirit. No wonder Paul said, "*I speak in tongues more than all of you*" (1 Corinthians 14:18).

### ASSURANCE

Who has not been attacked in their mind as to their acceptance by the Lord? Such thoughts as: 'Are you sure you are born again?', 'You are not really saved!', and 'God has rejected you!', are part of Satan's strategy to undermine Christians and bring them into the bondage of fear and despair. Speaking out in tongues can be a powerful defense against such an attack and can silence the tormenting voice of the 'accuser'.

In the Gospel of John are recorded these words of Jesus:

*I will ask the Father, and he will give you another Counselor to be with you for ever – the Spirit of truth. The world cannot accept him, because it neither sees him nor knows him. But you know him, for he lives with you and will be in you* (John 14:16-17).

Speaking in tongues is evidence of the indwelling Holy Spirit. The world – those outside of Christ – are not able to receive Him. So when a believer comes under attack as to his position in Christ, he can simply let pour forth praise and worship to the Lord in other tongues. In effect, he is saying to the accuser, "Listen, Satan, this is the evidence that the Holy Spirit abides in me – that I am a child of God – so stop your insinuations and go!"

This links in with Paul's encouragement to the Romans:

*For you did not receive a spirit that makes you a slave again to fear, but you received the Spirit of sonship. And by him we cry, 'Abba, Father'. The Spirit himself testifies with our spirit that we are God's children* (Romans 8:15, 16).

The Holy Spirit has come to be to us all that Jesus was to the disciples. He is the Comforter, and as we allow Him space, He will be the strengthener we need. To exercise the gift of tongues opens the way for the Holy Spirit to move in.

### SPIRITUAL REFRESHING

Who has not experienced a time of dryness in their Christian walk? A time when it takes an effort to pray or to read the Word of God. A time when following the Lord seems like hard work. Men of God in the Scriptures had such experiences. Elijah, fearing for his life, ran from Ahab's evil queen, Jezebel (1 Kings 19:1-8). He even prayed for death: *"I have had enough, Lord. Take my life; I am no better than my ancestors."* He needed refreshing from the Lord, and an angel came and ministered to him.

At one time in his life King David was an outlaw hunted by King Saul. He was a young man who had known the Lord's protection and the anointing of the Holy Spirit. He had even had God's promise for the future, yet he thought to himself, *"One of these days I shall be destroyed by the hand of Saul"* (1 Samuel 27:1). The pressures of being a fugitive had sapped his spiritual strength.

The Apostle Paul, writing to the church at Corinth, tells how he and his companions suffered hardship. They were "under great pressure, far beyond their

ability to endure, so that they despaired even of life"
(2 Corinthians 1:8).

In such times, we need a supernatural refreshing. Jesus said to the Samaritan woman He met at the well that He could give living water to those who asked Him (John 4:10). Later, to a seeking multitude at the great Jewish festival of the Feast of Tabernacles, He spoke of *'streams of living water flowing from within'* (John 7:38). John, who recorded these words of Jesus, then makes it clear that this living water is the indwelling presence of the Holy Spirit. Speaking in tongues, worshipping and praising the Lord, releases the streams of living water, causing the fountain to bubble up, and this brings refreshing in all times of dryness. God, in His wisdom and mercy, has given us the Comforter – the Holy Spirit – to refresh us. When we are spiritually dry, it is often an effort to begin to praise the Lord, yet it is an effort that brings forth the streams of living water.

### HEALTH AND UNDERSTANDING

The Holy Spirit is able to strengthen and restore us physically.

*If the Spirit of him who raised Jesus from the dead is living in you, he who raised Christ from the dead will also give life to your mortal bodies through his Spirit, who lives in you.* (Romans 8:11)

This passage, which reveals the hope of resurrection from the dead for the Christian, also holds a promise of life and healing now. To worship and pray in the Spirit – that is, in other tongues – is a way of letting the Holy Spirit do His work of healing and restoration. As Christians, we need to give place to the Spirit of Life to quicken us physically. In much the same way, because the Holy Spirit is the Spirit of truth and of wisdom, He is able to quicken our minds, bringing insight and revelation, and, when necessary, bringing back Scripture to our memory. Indeed, by quickening our minds, it is possible for the Holy Spirit to impart to us natural wisdom and sound judgment.

*For God has not given us a spirit of fear, but of power and of love and of a sound mind* (2 Timothy 1:7 NKJV).

Keeping filled with the Spirit provides the opportunity the Comforter needs to forward His work in us. The command in Ephesians 5:18 *"to be filled with the Spirit"* is followed with a word on how we can do this: *"Speak to one another with psalms, hymns and spiritual songs. Sing and make music in your heart to the Lord."* Spiritual songs include 'singing in the Spirit' in other tongues.

CHAPTER 4

# THE VALUE OF TONGUES TO THE INDIVIDUAL BELIEVER: PART 2

**LEARNING TO CONTROL OUR TONGUE**

The epistle of James has a section dealing with the need Christians have to tame their tongues (James 3:1-12). As Christians, we need to learn wholesome speech. We need to speak out words of encouragement, blessing and praise, and not utter that which is destructive, critical or vicious. James likens the tongue to a careless spark that can set a forest ablaze or the rudder that looks so small and yet can turn a large ship. He goes on to explain that our tongue needs to be trained, so that when we speak, we will be as a fountain pouring forth only pure, fresh water.

Curses and blasphemy so readily pour out from those who are in the world. They come from the tongue so effortlessly, as if without thought. Demons seek to control and use the tongue to cause strife and hurt.

We need to bring our tongues under the control of the Holy Spirit. As we make a daily practice of using our gift of tongues for worship and prayer, it becomes part of our nature. Just as you suddenly discover yourself humming a tune or singing a song without any real conscious effort, so we will find it natural and easy to worship, sing and pray in tongues at all times.

We can retrain and discipline our tongue for the kingdom of God. It is significant that the first thing that evidenced the disciples having received the Holy Spirit was that the Holy Spirit used their tongues in praise. The member of our body *"no man can tame,"* as James describes it, can yield to the sweet restraint of the Spirit of God. At first, it may be an effort to speak out in tongues, but as we make that effort, over-coming our own reluctance and any spiritual oppo-sition, we are training our tongue for righteousness. Just as David, in Psalm 144, claims that God trains his hands for war, so the Holy Spirit masters our tongue for the King's service.

### SPEAKING IN TONGUES STIMULATES FAITH

There are times when, as Christians seeking to serve the Lord, we are called upon to meet a challenge, respond to a need, or pray for someone in distress or sickness, and we feel inadequate or weak in faith ourselves at that moment. It is then that the Holy Spirit is ready to quicken our faith as we call on Him. In my experience, simply to worship the Lord in tongues has the effect of overcoming tiredness, and it releases a surge of confi-dence. The Holy Spirit helps our faith level to rise. Paul encouraged Timothy to *"stir up the gift of God which is in you*" (2 Timothy 1:6 NKJV). The Holy Spirit is the One who can encourage and promote faith in us. A time of praise in tongues is the opportunity He needs to prepare us.

All we do for the Lord needs faith. We preach and believe God will confirm His Word in the hearts of the hearers by faith; we pray for the sick by faith; we cast out demons by faith; and we prophesy by faith. Without faith it is impossible to please God (Hebrews 11:6). For preachers, a time spent praying and offering up praises to God in other tongues before ministering to God's people is always valuable, because faith is quickened.

For those who have come to "receive" – either to hear the Word of God preached or to receive healing or counsel – praying in tongues beforehand is good preparation, because they need to "receive" by faith.

## MAINTAINING AN ENVIRONMENT OF CALM AND REST

Christians are often in what could be called a "hostile environment" where the lifestyle, the conversation and attitude of those around them create a constant undermining pressure.

While living in Sodom, Lot was distressed by the filthy lives of the lawless men he saw around him, and he was anguished by what he saw and heard (2 Peter 2:6-8). The presence of believers in such an atmosphere can bring a change. We can be as a sweet fragrance by being there – by what we do and also by the effect of our words. Speaking in tongues increases the awareness of the Holy Spirit's presence. We bring a spiritual freshness, overcoming the sour atmosphere of ugliness. Just as the light shines in the darkness, scattering the night (see John 1:5), so the words of the Holy Spirit on our lips scatter the deadness of this world.

We are called to be salt and light in this world-- not to be overcome, but to be overcomers. We are to reign in life through Christ Jesus.

**GIVING THANKS TO GOD**

When the goodness of God towards us overwhelms our hearts, and we feel much like the songwriter who wrote, "Jesus, your love has melted my heart," we want to praise and truly worship the One who has done so much for us. However, often we feel inadequate in expressing our love. Our words, our language, are not enough. It is then that the Holy Spirit can come to our aid. As we worship the Lord in the language inspired by the Holy Spirit, it becomes the "perfection of praise." Paul, in 1 Corinthians 14:16, writes of *"praising God with your spirit."* This is what the disciples were doing on the day of Pentecost, when the Holy Spirit was first poured out on the believers. The wondering crowd who ran together said, *"We hear them declaring the wonders of God"* (Acts 2:11). Such worship in the spirit gladdens the Father's heart. Jesus has said that the Father seeks those who will worship Him in spirit and in truth (John 4:23-24).

There is repeated encouragement in the Psalms for us to praise the Lord. For example:

Psalm 107:1 *Give thanks to the Lord, for He is good.*
Psalm 144:1 *Praise be to the Lord, my Rock.*
Psalm 146:1 *Praise the Lord, O my soul.*
Psalm 149:1 *Praise the Lord. Sing to the Lord a new song.*

We may sing in tongues to the Lord, and truly this will be a *"new song."* This is probably what Paul is referring to in 1 Corinthians 14:15, when he writes, *"I will sing with my spirit"*. It is a tremendous experience to be in a congregation who are "singing in the spirit" and to sense/feel the powerful anointing that comes at such times.

When Paul and Silas were at Philippi, they were accused of causing an uproar in the city and, as a result, they were flogged at the command of the magistrates and then put in jail (Acts 16:23). At midnight, they were in pain and their feet were in stocks, and yet they prayed and sang. I am sure that this was one of the occasions when Paul "sang in the spirit," opening up his heart to God and exercising the gift of tongues.

The Holy Spirit's work is to *"testify to Jesus"* (John 15:25). As we sing out in tongues, we let Him sing out the victory and majesty of Jesus through our lips.

Paul and Silas were not long in the darkness of the inner prison. The midnight prayer and praise time brought a dramatic change. The building was shaken by an earthquake. As a result, the doors of the prison swung open, yet, to the amazement of the jailer, not one prisoner left his cell. That night salvation came to the jailer and his household, and Paul and Silas were freed from the prison. Praise brought the victory.

We should become people who praise God continually. Such offerings gladden the Father's heart. Let praising God in other tongues become for you a lifestyle.

**CHAPTER 5**

# THE USE OF THE GIFT OF TONGUES IN PRAYER

**PRAYING IN LINE WITH THE LORD'S WILL**

There are instances in the life of every Christian when there is an uncertainty as to what to pray for and how to pray. The Holy Spirit, who knows all things, is present and able to help us in times such as this. Paul expresses it this way:

*The Spirit helps us in our weakness. We do not know what we ought to pray, but the Spirit himself intercedes for us with groans that words cannot express. And he who searches our hearts knows the mind of the Spirit, because the Spirit intercedes for the saints in accordance with God's will.* (Romans 8:26-27)

To pray in tongues in these difficult situations fulfills the command of Jesus that *"men ought always to pray, and not to faint"* (Luke 18:1 AV). It also gives the assurance that comes from interceding in the Spirit – that is, the knowledge, the settled conviction, that *"in all things God works for the good of those who love him"* (Romans 8:28).

Prayer opens the way for the will of God to be realized in our lives. Jesus taught us to pray: *"Father... Thy Kingdom come. Thy will be done in earth, as it is in heaven"* (Matthew 6:10 AV).

Praying in the Spirit helps bring in God's kingdom, where His righteousness rules.

**PRAYING FOR THAT WHICH IS UNKNOWN**

Prayer opens the way for the kingdom of God and the power of God to be demonstrated in the lives of men and women. The angels of God stand ready to intervene on behalf of the children of God. However, God, in His wisdom, has ordained that it is when men call upon Him that He will answer.

The Word of God encourages Christians to pray for one another, and by prayer and intercession to bring the blessing and protection of the Lord into the lives of other people. Paul constantly prayed for the early Church, and he often asked other believers to pray for him. For example, he asked the Ephesian church to *"pray also for me, that whenever I open my mouth, words may be given me so that I will fearlessly make known the mystery of the gospel"* (Ephesians 6:19).

The Holy Spirit seeks to encourage this prayer of support. At times, He will bring a strong impression to the mind of a believer, indicating that someone they know is in need. William Burton, a pioneer missionary to the then-Belgian Congo, tells of how he had been very close to death on one of his journeys through the African bush, and of how he was healed and immediately set free from a fever as the power of God touched his body. Later, while visiting a church in England, a Christian sister told him how one night she was awakened with an impression that she needed to pray for Mr. Burton. She then immediately began to pray in English and in other tongues until the burden she had felt to pray lifted. That time of intercession was just the moment in which the missionary was in such great need.

Children of God are to be led by the Spirit of God and be aware of such prompting of the Holy Spirit to pray. At times, the circumstances of the need will not be known, and there will be no way of finding out, yet the Holy Spirit knows all things and can be relied upon to help. He will enable direct, pertinent intercession to be made if we speak forth in other tongues.

Ida Mae Hammond, who with her husband is involved in teaching spiritual warfare and deliverance in many countries, tells of how, just prior to the critical events that took place in Poland in the early 1980's, she began to intercede in a tongue that was new to her. The Holy Spirit showed her that she was interceding in Polish for that nation. Later, the Lord opened the way for her, together with me and her husband, Frank, to visit that country for seminars on spiritual warfare.

A further example of intercession in other tongues was

given by Miss Grace Carroll, a long-time employee at the International Headquarters of the Assemblies of God. For many years, she was secretary to Ralph M. Riggs, while he served as district superintendent of the Southern Missouri District, assistant general superintendent of the Assemblies of God, and finally general superintendent.

The Assemblies of God, Southern Missouri camp grounds are located on the shore of the beautiful Lake of the Ozarks. After a camp-meeting sermon by Arthur Graves one morning in the summer of 1952, there lingered a special sense of the presence of the Holy Spirit. Many who came to the altar to pray ignored the dinner bell.

Grace Carroll remained at the altar praying with a heart burdened for the needs of those in her own family. As she prayed "in the Spirit," she little dreamed how far her prayers were reaching. Miss Carroll raised her head after the burden had lifted. She then noticed a small, dark-haired woman kneeling next to her. Tears were pouring down this woman's face, as, in broken English, she tried to say something.

Miss Carroll thought the woman was asking her to pray for her family, but the little woman said, "You don't understand. You were praying for my family. You were praying in the Croatian language (one of the languages spoken in Yugoslavia). You called out names of cities and villages that are well known to me. You were praying for the sick and the dying, those in hospitals, etc." She went on to say that she had frequently heard people in Pentecostal prayer meetings praying for Yugoslavia.

What unusual means God has of ministering to the needs of His people! Here was a Pentecostal praying, she thought, for her own family, yet her prayer 'in the Spirit' was spanning the oceans, and she was interceding for places and people of whom she had never heard. In this charismatic experience, we never really know how effective prayer can be.

Paul's encouragement is to *"pray in the Spirit on all occasions with all kinds of prayers and requests" (Ephesians* 6:18).

CHAPTER 6

# SPIRITUAL WARFARE AND THE GIFT OF TONGUES

*Our struggle is not against flesh and blood, but against the rulers, against the authorities, against the powers of this dark world and against the spiritual forces of evil in the heavenly realms.* (Ephesians 6:12)

This verse is a reminder that men and women are beset by the hostile agents of Satan's kingdom. Demonic powers and fallen angels that rule in the heavens over peoples and cities are pressuring and harassing, and seeking to ensnare God's children and hold up the onward sweep of the Kingdom of Righteousness (Ephesians 6:10-18). Followers of Christ are called to be active in this war by putting on the armor provided and entering into the "struggle." After listing the components of the Christian, spiritual armor – that is, the belt of truth, the breastplate of righteousness, feet fitted with the Gospel, the shield of faith, the helmet of salvation, and the sword of the Spirit – the command is to *"pray in the Spirit."*

Without revelation from the Lord, it is not always

possible to understand what powers are in operation against the believer. Often, we need to know who the *"strong man"* is, so that he can be bound and the spoils taken, thus allowing men and women to be rescued from the bondages of sickness, depression and sin (see Matthew 12:25-29). Speaking out in faith is the way the Word of God encourages us to take the offensive and overcome our adversary.

Psalm 149:6 describes the praise of God that we offer up as *"a double-edged sword"* in our hands. As we sing and shout out our praises, we are wielding that sword. By our praise, the kings are bound with fetters and nobles with shackles of iron. These are not human kings and potentates, but the satanic princes that rule in the heavens. The Prince of Persia, spoken of in Daniel 10, was just such a spirit ruler. His dominion over the Empire of Persia was broken when Daniel prayed. In a similar way, we can also render powerless the spiritual princes over cities and nations. In Revelation 1:11, the accuser, Satan, is overcome by *"the blood of the Lamb and by the word of their testimony"*. Again, the emphasis is on that which is spoken out in faith. Jesus said to His disciples, "*Speak to the mountain and it will be cast into the sea*" (Mark 11:23). Often in the Scriptures, a mountain is used as a figure of a powerful, dominant nation. In recent years, the mountain of the Russian communist power has been cast down. This has happened because men and women have prayed in faith, binding the strong man, and have often prayed in tongues, thus releasing the angels of God to the fight. Not knowing the identity of the opponent or the exact nature of his attack, the believer can look to the help of the Holy Spirit, and in other tongues speak out and bind the power of the enemy. Knowing you have this authority, you can speak out in faith.

Some years ago, I visited the town of Villach in Austria to hold a week of meetings in a Pentecostal church in the town. We were aware of strong spiritual opposition to the gospel as soon as we arrived at the church. Encouraged by a word of prophesy, four of us – the three visitors from England and the local pastor – went up one of the mountains which are around the town. There we entered into spiritual warfare against the strong man – the spiritual powers of Satan that sought to control the area. Battling in prayer, two of us had a strange experience as we stood on a cliff edge looking out over the homes and the river below. We both had an urge to throw ourselves forward over the cliff, which would have been suicide. Stepping back, I remember rebuking and resisting the attack of the enemy in other tongues, and the uncanny sensation passed. That week we had a breakthrough in that church. Local Austrians were saved, and there were physical healings, demons were cast out, and a number of the fellowship were baptized in the Holy Spirit. We could only speculate as to the demonic powers at work in that place, but the Holy

Spirit enabled us to effectively resist them by praying in the Spirit.

## CHAPTER 7

# HOW TO RECEIVE
# THE GIFT OF TONGUES

I believe that all who have received the baptism in the Holy Spirit have the ability to speak in tongues. This was the disciples' experience on the day of Pentecost. If you are a believer in Jesus – a child of God by faith in the Lord Jesus – you should seek to be filled with the Holy Spirit. Ask the Father to fill you.

*Repent and be baptized, every one of you, in the name of Jesus Christ so that your sins may be forgiven. And you will receive the gift of the Holy Spirit.*
(Acts 2:38)

Jesus said, *"If you then though you are evil, know how to give good gifts to your children, how much more will your Father in heaven give the Holy Spirit to those who ask him."*
(Luke 11:13)

Jesus also said, *"If a man is thirsty, let him come to me and drink. Whoever believes in me, as the Scripture has*

*said, stream of living water will flow from within him."*
(John 7:37, 38)

If you ask the Father, believing His promise, He will fill you with His Holy Spirit. You then have to begin to speak out in faith the words the Holy Spirit will give to you. Some people anticipate that the Holy Spirit will take over their tongues and vocal chords – that they are taken over by the Spirit. It is true that some people feel a greater anointing than others when they first speak in tongues, but they are never out of control. It is our choice as to whether we speak out the words of praise that the Holy Spirit gives to us. It may be that we need to overcome a natural reluctance to do something that seems foolish or strange to our mind. Those people who have experienced a block in finding freedom to worship in tongues may need to seek deliverance from evil spirits which hinder. After an evening service, on a ministry trip I took to Poland in 1979, I was fellowshipping with a group of young people from the church. A young woman, who was a university student in the town, had started attending the church. Her home church, in another part of Poland, was opposed to speaking in tongues and the gifts of the Holy Spirit, which they believed had ceased in the Apostles' time. Convinced by what she had seen and heard, she asked us to pray for her for the infilling of the Holy Spirit and the gift of tongues. When we prayed, she said she felt as if there were something within that was blocking her. I prayed and commanded any spirit that had come with wrong teaching, any demon that was hindering her, to leave. At once, she was set free, and she began to worship God fluently in other tongues.

A lady of over 80 years of age came forward in a meeting in Austria and told me that she had been seeking the gift of the Holy Spirit since she was saved some 20 years before. I laid hands on her and prayed for her to be filled, but there was evidently no response. She then told me that, before becoming a Christian, she had been involved in the occult and fortune telling. I prayed again, commanding all occult spirits to leave her. She gave a deep sigh and then began to praise God in other tongues. If former involvement in the occult is holding you back from receiving the infilling of the Holy Spirit or hindering your fluency in the gift of tongues, then pray to God. Renounce the occult, freeing yourself from demonic powers in the name of Jesus. Expel any spirit that hinders you, and then receive the infilling of the Holy Spirit and begin to worship God in tongues by faith. Do not be discouraged by any initial lack of fluency in the gift. As you continue to use what God has given, the tongues will develop and the richness of the gift will become evident.

CHAPTER 8

# THE USE OF TONGUES IN THE CHURCH

### THE GIFT OF TONGUES IN A PUBLIC MEETING

The private or individual use of tongues is generally from the spirit of the man godward. When the gift is used in a public meeting, it is quite often from God to man. This manifestation of tongues, plus the interpretation, is equivalent to prophecy (cf 1 Corinthians 11:5). The guiding principle of all public manifestations of the inspirational gifts should be that the believers in the Church are edified (cf 1 Corinthians 14:3-5, 12, 17, 26). Paul, in 1 Corinthians 14:19, explains what he means by "edifying:" *"I would rather speak... to instruct others."* Later, in verse 31 of the same chapter, he goes on to say, *"that everyone may be instructed and encouraged."*

The receiving of divine truth into our hearts and minds is what we need to build us up in the faith.

It would seem that the church in Corinth had rather disorderly meetings. Many people were speaking out in tongues, possibly without any interpretation, and there were also many prophecies being given. To bring order and to restore a healthy balance to the public use of the gifts of the Spirit, Paul set out guidelines that we should seek to follow in our local churches.

(a) A "message in tongues" should always be followed by an interpretation. In a New Testament fellowship, generally there will be a number of brothers and sisters who exercise the gift of interpretation of tongues. If it is known that there is no one present who can interpret, and the one desiring to bring the message in tongues does not have the faith to bring an interpretation to the tongue him/herself, it would be better not to give the tongue. *"If there is no interpreter, the speaker should keep quiet in the church and speak to himself and God"* (1 Corinthians 14:28).

(b) Messages in tongues should be limited to two or three in a gathering. *"If any one speaks in a tongue, two – or at the most three – should speak, one at a time, and someone must interpret"* (1 Corinthians 14:27).

It is necessary that teaching is given to the people of God, so that the correct use of the gift is understood. If someone with excess zeal or someone who is not aware of the guidelines of Scripture speaks in tongues or prophesies, when it would have been better if they had not, they should be treated with grace and care, and made aware of their mistake. However, this should not be done in a way that would humiliate or wound. A private word of encouragement is probably the best way to tackle this.

## ONE INTERPRETER

Paul's advice in 1 Corinthians 14, verse 27, is that there should be only two or three messages in tongues in a meeting, and that one person at a time should speak and *"someone must interpret."* This should not be taken to mean that the one person should interpret all the tongues which have been given. Of course, this may indeed happen, but Paul's meaning here is that each tongue should have only one person interpreting that tongue. It is possible to have three tongues given and three different persons interpreting those tongues.

## CAN I GIVE A MESSAGE IN TONGUES?

If you desire the Holy Spirit to use you to bring a message in tongues to the Church, then tell the Lord that this is how you want Him to use you. Then, when you gather with the fellowship you belong to, have an attitude of heart which anticipates that the Lord will use you.

As you feel the leading of God's Spirit – the anointing of God upon you – wait for an opportunity in the service for you to bring the message in tongues. When the Holy Spirit directs a gathering of believers, He can cause periods of quiet or calm when the gifts can be exercised, just as a conductor quietens the instruments in an orchestra to bring in a soloist. When you give out the tongue, speak clearly and in a way that will be evident to all present that you are giving a message for the Church. When you have delivered what you feel the Holy Spirit is urging you to give, then stop. Be careful not to overrun what the Holy Spirit intends, to repeat what has just been given, or to peter out into words of praise in other tongues. If your church or fellowship is unsure about the public exercise of the gifts of the Spirit, ask those responsible for the oversight of the church if they have any objection to your using spiritual gifts and giving a message in tongues.

If your church does not accept that the gift of tongues should be used in public worship, it would be wrong of you to impose the use of your gift on them. Rather than bringing blessing, it would bring anger and division. Far better to pray that God will open their hearts to what the Holy Spirit is doing in the world or, alternatively, seek fellowship where the gifts of the Spirit are accepted.

**THE GIFT OF INTERPRETATION OF TONGUES**

This companion gift to speaking in tongues enables the one with the gift to interpret the tongue that is spoken into the language of those people present. The interpreter himself does not understand the tongue spoken, but the Holy Spirit in him does, and he speaks out the interpretation by the inspiration of the Holy Spirit.

The interpretation of tongues, then, comes forth in the same way as prophecy.

The inspiration can come in various ways to the one who interprets. Some people have a phrase that comes to them, and as they speak it out, the rest of the message comes forth. Others receive a mental vision when the tongue is given, and they describe it, or what it represents, to the congregation.

The interpretation can come forth under a strong anointing or be given rather hesitantly. This depends on the one interpreting. Fear or anxiety often impedes the flow of the gift. We need to pray for rich anointing. The interpreter should be encouraged to seek God and to develop his/her gift.

There is a concern expressed, at times, where there seems to be a great difference between the length of the utterance in tongues and the interpretation, which follows. However, it must be borne in mind that we are dealing with an interpretation and not a translation. The message conveyed may have been given more or less graphically than the tongue spoken out, or the tongue may have had a degree of repetition, or the interpretation could have been lengthened by repetition. The interpretation may also move into a prophecy, the tongue being the encouragement or spur to the prophetic gift being exercised.

I was once attending an induction service for a new pastor in a church in South London, and I had a word of prophecy which I was reluctant to give. It was a warning of a shaking which was to come to that church, and it would have cut across the way the service was being led. I remember praying hard: "If you want me to give this word, let someone speak in tongues and I'll speak out the message as an interpretation." I wanted confirmation from the Holy Spirit that I was in tune with what He wanted. As soon as I had framed that prayer in my heart, someone spoke out a message in tongues, and I gave the word the Lord wanted me to bring. It had a very sobering effect on the meeting, but some months later, the new pastor confirmed the truth of what was foretold that afternoon.

The testing of prophecy and not despising the prophetic gift applies equally to the gift of interpretation of tongues. If you seek to speak in tongues, seek to interpret, so that you may be a greater blessing to the Church.

**PERSONAL RESPONSIBILITY**

The Holy Spirit inspires the words when we speak in tongues. However, the speaker remains responsible for the way the words are expressed, because it is his choice to speak out in tongues or not. Just as the tone of one's voice will alter with the circumstances when speaking one's own language (as will the forcefulness or softness of the words expressed), so the speaker in tongues modifies the way he expresses his gift.

When speaking words of endearment to a wife or comfort and encouragement to a child, the voice is soft and gentle, especially when this is compared with the volume and perhaps the harshness needed to chase away a stray dog from the garden. Entering into spiritual warfare in tongues often requires a forcefulness and aggression, whereas tongues in worship tend to have a greater gentleness or sweetness. We are to use wisdom with the manifestation of the gifts.

At times, however, an urgency from the Holy Spirit comes through into the way we express the gift of tongues. Generally though, the speaker chooses how he will speak.

Some years ago, a sister in our fellowship had the habit of raising the pitch of her voice to a level that caused concern and embarrassment whenever she gave a message in tongues. After a word of counsel, the sister modified her delivery when she spoke in tongues, thus making her gift much more acceptable. How she spoke had always been under her control. This was a mannerism which required correction.

The Holy Spirit has not come to dominate men and women, but to be our Helper. John calls the Holy Spirit the *"Comforter."* This is translated from the Greek word *"Paraclete,"* which means *"one who comes alongside to help."* The believer is always in control when exercising the gifts of the Holy Spirit. He never forces anyone to do anything against his or her will; hence Paul's statement in 1 Corinthians 14:32: *"the spirits of prophets are subject to the control of prophets".*

If someone interrupts a meeting with an utterance in tongues, perhaps cutting across another who is praying or even preaching, such an interruption is out of order and shows bad manners or a lack of self-discipline on the part of the one speaking in tongues. To claim "the Spirit made me do it" would not be true. That is why Paul writes that messages in tongues in a public meeting should be limited to two or three, and if there is no one to interpret, the speaker should keep quiet (1 Corinthians 14:27, 28). From this, it is evident that the speaker has the power to refrain from speaking out.

CHAPTER 9

# QUESTIONS WHICH ARE SOMETIMES ASKED ABOUT TONGUES

This section seeks to answer some of the questions which are asked concerning speaking in tongues.

### 1. Can the Devil Understand Us When We Speak in Tongues?

Some people maintain that when we speak in tongues in prayer or praise to God, we, by the Holy Spirit, are communicating with the Lord in a secret language that the enemy cannot understand. This is not an issue about which we should be too dogmatic. As I see it, the Holy Spirit, who inspires the language spoken, can choose to use a tongue that no demon or any of Satan's kingdom could understand, or He may speak in a tongue that they know well, perhaps filling them with dread and consternation.

Paul, in his first epistle to the Corinthians, refers to the tongues of men and angels (see 1 Corinthians 13:1). This would suggest that we can even, by the Holy Spirit, speak to fallen angels in their own tongue, should that be what the Holy Spirit desires.

## 2.   Are All Tongues Directed Only to God?

Part of the instruction to the church at Corinth in-
cludes the statement: *"Anyone who speaks in a tongue
does not speak to men but to God"* (1 Corinthians 14:2).
This verse has been taken by some to mean that the gift
of tongues should always be directed to God. Further,
that any interpretation of that tongue which is not a
form of speech directly addressed to God is unscrip-
tural. This would be interpreting this passage in a way
Paul never intended.

Paul is asking for balance and wisdom in the public
gatherings of the church at Corinth, because the Christians there had become rather extreme in their public
use of the gift of tongues. His point here is concerned
with understanding the tongue. If the Church is to be
edified, encouraged or comforted, those present must
understand what is said. If we speak in tongues only, it
is *"to God,"* because only God can understand the utterance. As we have already seen, tongues can be directed
other than to God.

There are also instances of a person speaking in tongues
when there has been someone present whose own language has been spoken out, and the Holy Spirit had
spoken directly to that person (Acts 2:5-12).

My father was once attending a convention meeting
in Central London in the 1930's, and a girl of about
twelve years of age spoke in tongues. The language she
spoke in was a Chinese dialect recognized by a Chinese

Christian present. He testified before the congregation what he had heard and how God had spoken to him in that utterance.

The following are examples of tongues which were directly addressed to those people who could understand the language used. "God Told Him Where to Go" and "God Knew Their Names" are taken from a book of such incidents compiled by Ralph W. Harris under the title, *Spoken by the Spirit*.

### i. Tongues Used to Bless and Restore:

Stanley Frodsham, in his book *Spirit Filled, Taught and Led*, relates the experience of a missionary to India, who on furlough in the U.S.A. was a guest at the home of a Mrs. Montgomery of Oakland, California. Mrs. Montgomery was concerned by how weak and emaciated her visitor looked, and filled with compassion, she laid hands on her guest and prayed. As she prayed, she began to speak in tongues. The missionary look up in surprise and said, "Why, you are speaking Hindustani (a language Mrs. Montgomery did not know) and you are saying:" "Take, my beloved, take." From that time on, health and strength began to return to the weak missionary, and in a few months she was restored.

### ii. God Told Him Where to Go:

In the summer of 1925, Yourish Neesan, an evangelist from the country of Persia (now known as Iran), was conducting services in a church on Ingleside Terrace in Kalamazoo, Michigan. Under his ministry, many seekers after God received the Pentecostal experience. Among those filled with the Spirit was Mrs. Bessie Cooley.

During one of the services, Mrs. Cooley gave an utterance in other tongues. She recalled that several times the word 'Hamadan' was spoken. At the conclusion of the service, the evangelist talked to Mrs. Cooley and asked her if she had understood what she was saying under the anointing of the Holy Spirit. Of course, she hadn't. He then told her that the message had been in the Persian language and had been directed to him. God had told him to return to Persia and that there would be an open door of ministry in the city of Hamadan!

Not long after this incident, Yourish Neesan returned to his native land and began ministering to his own people. A communication from him some time later stated that he had indeed opened a mission in the city of Hamadan, and that it was prospering.

The source of this account was Everett D. Cooley, son of Mrs. Bessie Cooley, who is now retired and living in Springfield, Missouri, after serving as a pastor and as district superintendent of the Assemblies of God for the State of Michigan.

### iii. God Knew Their Names:

Robert Blumm has come a long way. Born in New York City, he early became a member of one of the gangs that roamed the streets seeking to take vengeance on a society that they hated. At the age of thirteen, he began taking drugs; and by the time he was sixteen, he was an addict. No one seemed to care for him, and the God he only faintly knew about seemed very remote.

Dropping out of school, he joined the Army, vaguely hoping to find some meaning in life. He was assigned to combat duty in Vietnam in 1966-67. Here, fortunately, he became acquainted with two young Christian soldiers, who led him to a saving knowledge of Jesus Christ in May, 1967. That same night, he experienced a further demonstration of the power of the gospel: he received immediate deliverance from his drug habit. Bob Blumm learned that God had additional blessings for him in the experience known as the baptism in the Holy Spirit. Three months after his conversion, he was filled with the Spirit and spoke with other tongues as the Spirit gave him utterance. He says, "Now I had a language to speak to God with and the added blessing of power to preach the message of Christ crucified, risen, and coming again." (Of course, God understands English too!)

Blumm often slipped away when off duty to find a secret place to pray. One night, after treating mass casualties, he left the surgical hospital to take his heavy burden to the Lord. As he felt the presence of the Holy Spirit around him, he began praying fervently in an unknown tongue.

After praying for some time, Bob felt the burden lift. At the same time, he sensed the presence of someone behind him. Looking around, he saw two Vietnamese civilian workers. From time to time over a two-month period, they had observed him as he prayed. They told him that when he had prayed this time, he had prayed in the Vietnamese language. Through him, the Holy Spirit had addressed them by their names, Moui and Tinh. The Spirit had called on them to receive salvation and the same gift that they had observed in the life of Robert Blumm.

Both Vietnamese men received Christ as Savior that night. Robert Blumm is now an Assemblies of God minister, and at the time of writing, was C.A. (youth) director for the Long Island Section of the New York District. The source of this incident was Robert M. Blumm, Long Island, New York.

The gift of tongues is a sign to unbelievers.

### 3. What About Demonically Inspired Tongues?

The gifts of the Holy Spirit are, at times, counterfeited by demonic powers. In my experience of normal church life, these evil manifestations are not very common. Being over-cautious and suspicious of spiritual gifts in operation just because the gifts are sometimes counterfeited should be avoided. It is when people have had an involvement with the occult or false religion that such counterfeits are more likely to occur.

One of the gifts of the Holy Spirit is *"the discerning of spirits."* It is the Holy Spirit dwelling within us who will make us sensitive and aware of any tongue (or other spiritual gift) which is demonically inspired. When someone speaks in tongues by the Holy Spirit, it is witnessed to by the Holy Spirit within us. We feel comfortable with that tongue. When it is not of God, the spiritual man or woman will have a warning in his or her spirit and not be comfortable with what they hear.

4. **Why Do Some People Have an Experience of Speaking in Tongues, But Do Not Continue to Use the Gift?**

The first experience of speaking in tongues that we have can be under a strong anointing of the Holy Spirit. Some people are reluctant to speak out again in tongues without that same awareness of anointing. However, we are encouraged in the Word of God to act in faith and not to be led by our feelings. Although it is common for a sense of anointing to accompany prayer in the Spirit, it is essential that we understand that the experience of speaking in tongues is always initiated by an act of faith on our part (Romans 12:6).

Certain Christian teachers have held that there is a difference between speaking in tongues as an initial sign or evidence of the baptism in the Holy Spirit, and what they understand to be a distinct and separate *"gift of tongues"* that is not given to all. This idea has hindered many believers from exercising the gift of tongues which they have already received, believing that they must await a further gift from God.

In my experience, I found that as I continued to speak out in faith, the tongues that I had been given when I was baptized in the Holy Spirit, developed and diversified. It was not another gift, but a growth in the understanding and use of what God had given me.

If you are one of those people who have spoken out only the once in tongues, realize that the Holy Spirit wants to continually inspire you to exercise the gift as you choose to speak out in faith. It is good practice to spend time each day praying and praising God in tongues.

### 5. In 1 Corinthians 12, Verse 30, Why Does Paul Ask the Question, *"Do All Speak in Tongues?"*

The point Paul is making in chapter 12 of 1 Corinthians is that the believers in the local church are to be seen as members of the same body. They have received the same Holy Spirit and are not to boast and claim superiority over their brothers and sisters in Christ who have received differing gifts from the Holy Spirit. He likens the different responsibilities and challenges in the Church to the parts of the body working together. In verse 29, he asks the people at Corinth, *"Are all apostles? Are all prophets? Are all teachers? Do all work miracles? Do all have gifts of healing? Do all speak in tongues? Do all in-*

*terpret?"* The answer, of course, is "no." Paul, thereby, demonstrates the diversity of the gifts in the body, the Church. Paul often uses this method to emphasize his teaching. However, to take this passage to mean that it is not God's will for all to speak in tongues is to force a meaning that was never intended. Such a conclusion would contradict the desire that Paul expresses in the same letter, where he writes, "*I would like every one of you to speak in tongues*" (1 Corinthians 14:5). The Holy Spirit, through Paul, would not encourage us to desire that which was not available to us.

The question *"Do all speak in tongues?"* is in the context of the life of the local church, particularly when the church comes together for worship. It is the public use of tongues that Paul refers to here. In any congregation of Christians, there will be those who would not seek to exercise the gift of tongues. We could say, "Do all pray in the church and so lead the congregation in prayer?" Of course, there are many people who never pray in this way. However, it would be wrong to suppose that they cannot do it, because it is not God's will.

## 6. Why are Some Messages in Tongues Not Interpreted?

There can be a number of reasons for this. There may be no one present with the gift of interpretation of tongues, or the one giving the message in tongues may not have the faith to seek the interpretation or be aware that they should look to the Lord for the interpretation. Also, there may be those present with the gift of interpretation, but they feel no anointing or are in the wrong attitude of heart at the time. As the body of Christ, we are dependent on one another and have a responsibility to be ready for the work God has empowered us to do for Him.

# A LIST OF SCRIPTURES
# THAT REFER TO TONGUES

| | |
|---|---|
| Isaiah 28:11 | A prophecy predicting tongues (see 1 Corinthians 14:11) |
| Mark 16:17 | The promise of Jesus |
| Acts 2:4<br>Acts 2:11 | The Day of Pentecost |
| Acts 10:46 | The house of Cornelius |
| Acts 19:6 | Paul at Ephesus |
| 1 Corinthians 12:1<br>1 Corinthians 14:40 | Paul's teaching to the church at Corinth |

To pray "in the Spirit" is not exclusively praying in tongues. We can pray in our own tongue by the inspiration of the Holy Spirit (i.e. prophetic prayer). However, praying in tongues is a valuable part of praying in the Spirit (see Romans 8:26, 27; Ephesians 6:18).

# ABOUT THE AUTHOR

For over 40 years *John Edwards* was the pastor of New Life Christian Center Croydon in South London. Under his leadership, the church grew from a small community of forty Christians to well over a thousand members. John is a sought-after Bible teacher who has taught on the supernatural and deliverance across Europe. One of his desires is to see believers equipped to minister deliverance in the context of the local church.  John is married and has seven children. Together with his wife Doris, they have taken in and cared for more than 150 foster children over the years.

Johann Christoph Blumhardt

# JESUS IS VICTOR!

## Blumhardt's Battle with the Powers of Darkness

### Forwords by Kevin Dedmon & Walter Heidenreich

More gripping than Frank E. Peretti and Stephen King, this book written by Johann Christoph Blumhardt in 1844 is not a novel, but an enthralling eye-witness account sent to the Senior Church Authorities of the Kingdom of Württemberg. The consequence of the events described was a powerful revival in which the whole village of Möttlingen, with only a few exceptions, was converted. A movement sprang up in which thousands of people were healed from physical sickness and released from spiritual bondage. The lame could walk, the blind could see and bread was multiplied. Even the King of Württemberg paid an anonymous visit to one of the Sunday services which often attracted up to two thousand people to the small country church in Möttlingen. In 1852 the Blumhardts moved as a family to Bad Boll, where they established a healing community to which people from all over Europe were drawn.

Blumhardt concluded that the in-breaking of the kingdom of God he had experienced in Möttlingen represented what Jesus had in store for the whole cosmos. Johann Christoph Blumhardt and his son Christoph Friedrich Blumhardt had a major influence on Theologians such as Karl Barth, Emil Brunner, Dietrich Bonhoeffer and Jürgen Moltmann.

Paperback, 100 pages
US $12.95

Order on Amazon or directly from the publisher:
www.awakenmedia.de
info@awakenmedia.de
Paperback & Kindle Edition: www.amazon.com

John Edwards

# LOOSE HIM AND LET HIM GO

## A Manual in Deliverance

"In my name they will drive out demons," Jesus said to his disciples as part of his missionary command in Mark 16:17.
But, how can we do this?
John Edwards answers this question from scripture and from his many years of experience in deliverance ministry.
This book provides guidance, based on God's Word, through which you can find the freedom you need – and become an instrument of deliverance for others.

For over 40 years John Edwards was the pastor of New Life Christian Center Croydon in South London.
Under his leadership, the church grew from a small community of forty Christians to well over a thousand members.
John is a sought-after Bible teacher who has taught on spiritual warfare and deliverance across Europe.
One of his desires is to see believers equipped to minister deliverance in the context of the local church.

John is married and has seven children. Together with his wife Doris, they have taken in and cared for more than one hundred and fifty foster children over the years.

Paperback, 56 pages
US $ 7.95

Order on Amazon or directly from the publisher:
www.awakenmedia.de
info@awakenmedia.de
Paperback & Kindle Edition: www.amazon.com

# NOTES